THESE ARE THE CANDLES

Five Candle Lighting Readings For Advent

Wayne L. Tilden

CSS Publishing Company, Inc., Lima, Ohio

THESE ARE THE CANDLES

ISBN 0-7880-0844-7

These Are The Candles

Five Readings For Advent

The following readings are each read from offstage as the accompanying Advent Candle is lit. Then an appropriate hymn or carol is sung by the choir or the congregation. The suggested song is just that, a suggestion. Allow yourself some leeway and creativity.

Advent Candle 1

The Candle Of The Angels

Offstage Voice #1 (Male or Female):

This is the first candle — the first Advent candle — the candle of the angels. It was we who delivered the Good News of the birth of the Messiah: first to Mary, his mother; then to Joseph, Mary's fiancé; and finally to shepherds who were watching their sheep, not expecting a thing.

God made us His messengers — messengers of a time to come which would become a time of peace for all of humankind who were in His favor.

We not only delivered the message, but we also worshiped and praised Him — the Son of God. "Glory to God in the highest! And on earth peace to all men with whom He is well pleased." Those were the words we sang that night, words of praise. We angels continually praise the newborn Savior. And all the earth praises His Name!

Suggested song: "Angels We Have Heard On High"

Advent Candle 2

The Candle Of The Shepherds

Offstage Voice #2 (Preferably Male):

This is the second candle — the second Advent candle — the candle of the shepherds. We, like many others, were waiting for the Messiah — the Redeemer — to come one day ... *some* day.

Nevertheless, we were surprised — no, shocked — to be told by God's Host of Heaven that the Messiah had been born unto us *this day* as a baby who would be our Savior, our Christ, and our Lord.

Our wonderment gave way to expediency and we left our job in the countryside to see this wonderful thing which had been announced to us.

When, at last, we found the newborn King in a stable, with His parents, we worshiped and praised Him. That was all that we had to give Him, our undying praise! Praise is all *any* of us can give to a King who is God.

Suggested song: "While Shepherds Watched Their Flocks By Night"

Advent Candle 3

The Candle Of The Magi

Offstage Voice #3 (Preferably Male):

This is the third candle — the third Advent candle — the candle of the magi. Each one of us, like our ancestors before us, had been watching for the sign in the skies which would betoken the birth of the Jewish Messiah who was to become the Savior of the world.

We traveled to the west on a trip which led us to the Jewish capital city of Jerusalem, where King Herod's Wise Men directed us to the nearby village of Bethlehem. It was there that we found the young child with His mother, Mary. We presented Him with gifts which spoke of His destiny: gold — riches meant for the King; frankincense — a pleasing aroma to present to God; and myrrh — a burial spice — because His death and resurrection would be the salvation of all humankind.

We presented our gifts, and we praised Him. We praise Him still because He is still our King and our Lord and our Savior!

Suggested song: "We Three Kings Of Orient Are"

Advent Candle 4

The Candle Of Mary

Offstage Voice #4 (Female):

This is the fourth candle — the fourth Advent candle — the candle of Mary.

Who was I, a humble girl, that the Almighty God should look upon me with such favor? He revealed to me that I would be the one to bear His Son — His Son who would become the Savior of all humankind.

You have heard that Joseph and I had to travel many days to be counted in the Roman census at the city of our ancestors. You've heard that the night we arrived my Child was born with the animals in the stable of an inn. And you've surely heard that we were visited by a group of shepherds and later by wise kings from countries in the distant East.

Imagine! My Child — the Child given me by the Almighty God Himself — causing such a stir! As I contemplate all that my Child is, and all that He has done for humankind, I praise Him. I, His mother, praise Him for who He is and for everything He has done. I praise our Lord and our Savior. We all must praise Him!

Suggested song: "What Child Is This?"

Advent Candle 5

The Candle Of The Christ Child

Offstage Voice #5 (Male or Female, or Pastor):

This is the fifth candle — the fifth Advent candle — the candle of the Christ child.

Over the last four Sunday mornings we have heard Him praised through the words of the angels, the words of the shepherds, the words of the magi, and the words of His mother, Mary. In their own ways they each praised Him.

Now, on this eve of the celebration of His birth, we, too, praise Him for all that He has done for each one of us. We recognize the miracle of His birth to a virgin maiden; but more than that, we recognize the miracle of His saving Grace, offered for each one of us.

As we recognize His Gift to us, only then can we truly exclaim, "Jesus *is* worthy of praise! We *will* praise him with our *whole* lives, and through *all* of our days!" Yes, Jesus *is* worthy of our praise.

Suggested song: "Jesus Is Worthy Of Praise"

CPSIA information can be obtained
at www.ICGtesting.com
Printed in the USA
BVOW07s1423011217
501547BV00055B/241/P